Amazing Planet Earth

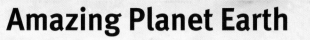

VIOLENT VOLCANOES

TERRY JENNINGS

W
FRANKLIN WATTS
LONDON • SYDNEY

 An Appleseed Editions book

First published in 2009 by Franklin Watts

Franklin Watts
338 Euston Road, London NW1 3BH

Franklin Watts Australia
Level 17/207 Kent St, Sydney, NSW 2000

© 2009 Appleseed Editions

Appleseed Editions Ltd
Well House, Friars Hill, Guestling, East Sussex TN35 4ET

Created by Q2AMedia
Book Editor: Michael Downey
Art Director: Rahul Dhiman
Designer: Ranjan Singh
Picture Researcher: Shreya Sharma
Line Artist: Sibi N. Devasia
Colouring Artist: Mahender Kumar

ISBN 978 0 7496 8803 5

Dewey classification: 551.21

All words in **bold** can be found in Glossary on pages 30–31.

Website information is correct at time of going to press. However, the publishers cannot
accept liability for any information or links found on third-party websites.

A CIP catalogue for this book is available from the British Library.

Picture credits
t=top b=bottom c=centre l=left r=right
Cover Image: Julien Grondin/ Shutterstock.
Back cover Image: Julien Grondin/ Shutterstock

Insides: Julien Grondin/ Shutterstock: Tittle Page, Seiden Allan/ Pacific Stock/ Photolibrary: 4, Supri Supri/ Reuters Pictures: 5t,
Donald A. Swanson/ USGS Photograph: 6b, Peter Lipman/ USGS Photograph: 6-7, Peter Lipman/ USGS Photograph: 8t, Dan Dzurisin/
USGS Photograph: 8b, Julien Grondin/ Shutterstock: 10b, The Natural History Museum/ Alamy: 11t, Russ Bishop/ Alamy: 12-13, J.D.
Griggs/ USGS Photograph: 13t, Enote/ Shutterstock: 15, K. Segerstrom/ US. Geological Survey: 16, US. Geological Survey: 17b, Jesús
Eloy Ramos Lara/ Dreamstime: 17t, Gregory Primo Photography/ Photographers Direct: 19t, National Geophysical Data Center: 18-19,
Jacques Langevin/ Corbis Sygma: 20b, Wessel du Plooy/ Shutterstock: 21t, Rick Hoblitt/ US. Geological Survey: 23t, US. Geological
Survey: 24, US. Geological Survey: 25, Peterm/ 123rf: 26, Zuki/ Istockphoto: 27, Peder Digre/ Shutterstock: 29
Q2AMedia Art Bank: 9, 10, 14, 22, 28.

Printed in China

Franklin Watts is a division of Hachette Children's Books,
an Hachette Livre UK company.
www.hachettelivre.co.uk

Contents

Violent volcanoes

The world's loudest noise was made not by an atomic bomb, but by a volcano. In 1883, there was a volcanic eruption on the uninhabited Indonesian island of Krakatoa. The eruption was so loud, that people 5,000 kilometres away in Australia heard the explosion. During the eruption, the land around Krakatoa shook so violently that nine gigantic ocean waves, or **tsunamis**, were formed. Huge, dark ash clouds also appeared. These clouds circled the Earth for many years, blocking out the Sun's warmth and lowering temperatures on the Earth's surface.

- Red-hot lava streams run down the sides of Kilauea, a volcano on the island of Hawaii. Kilauea has been erupting since 1983.

Liquid rock

Although volcanoes have differently shaped **cones**, all were formed from hot, liquid rock from deep inside the Earth. Scientists believe that there are 1,511 **active volcanoes** on land, and many more no longer active. Some volcanoes **erupt** violently, others are more quiet.

Heat and gases

Volcanoes play a vital part in forming islands, mountains and valleys, and in allowing unwanted heat and gases to escape from the Earth. Valuable rocks and minerals are also produced from **lava** and other volcanic material.

● Krakatoa, in Indonesia, is still very active. The volcano is seen here erupting in 2001.

DATA FILE

- There are many active volcanoes on the floor of the Earth's oceans.

- Most of the Earth's active volcanoes are found around the Pacific Ocean.

- The old township of Rabaul in Papua New Guinea, which was built inside a volcano, was destroyed in 1994 by ash from a volcanic eruption.

- About 600 million people live close to active volcanoes.

- Millions of people farm the fertile soils that form from volcanic ash.

- The most deadly volcanic eruption was that of Mount Tambora, in Indonesia, in 1815. This eruption resulted in 92,000 deaths.

Mount St Helens

Until May 1980, Mount St Helens stood 2,950 metres high in the Cascade Range in the northwest United States. The peak of the cone-shaped mountain was covered with snow. The land around, a national park, was popular with nature lovers and sightseers.

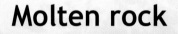

Molten rock

One day in May 1980, the sides of Mount St Helens began to split. Red-hot ash, lumps of molten rock and poisonous gas were shot more than 20 kilometres into the air.

Name: Mount St Helens
Location: Cascade Range, Washington State, USA
Height: 2,549 metres
Type: Composite cone
Eruption: 1980
Fatalities: 57

● Mount St Helens as it was before the explosive eruption in May 1980.

Shattered mountain

The eruption of Mount St Helens gave off energy equivalent to thousands of nuclear bombs. The explosion, which shattered part of the top of the mountain, was heard in Vancouver, Canada, about 320 kilometres away.

• Mount St Helens erupting in May 1980.

News Flash

Dateline 18 May 1980

The Mount St Helens volcano has now erupted and killed 57 people. A nearby town has been evacuated as the volcano sent flames, ash and black smoke to a height of more than 20,000 m. People living as far as 160 km away were thrown out of their beds by the force of the eruption.

Trees knocked down by the eruption of Mount St Helens. The temperatures were so high that the sap in the trees boiled.

Volcanic cloud

Hot gas, ash and rock from Mount St Helens flattened over ten million trees. A large chunk of the shattered mountain was swept into nearby Spirit Lake, causing waves 200 metres high. Two days later, the giant volcanic cloud that formed after the explosion had reached New York state. Within two weeks, the cloud had travelled around the world.

This car was buried in mud and lava 16 km away from Mount St. Helens.

Future danger

In September 2003, a new dome of solidified lava began to form inside Mount St Helens' **crater**. Today, this dome is as tall as an 80-storey building. In the future, it will totally fill the mountain and there will very probably be another huge eruption.

The moose return

Although many hundreds of moose died as a result of Mount St Helens' eruption in 1980, their numbers are now increasing again in the region.

DATA FILE

- The earthquake that started the May 1980 explosion reached 5.1 on the Richter Scale.

- The huge blast area covered about 600 sq. km.

- Millions of 200-year-old fir trees were flattened like matchsticks.

- Fast-moving gas clouds reached speeds of nearly 320 km/h.

- Hot ash shot more than 2,100 m into the air.

- The temperature of the nearby Toutle River rose to 90 °C.

BEFORE

- The peak of Mount St Helens was nearly a perfect cone shape.

AFTER

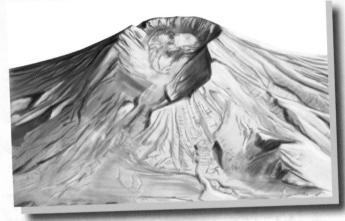

- The north side was blown apart, leaving a huge hole.

NOW

- The hole is slowly filling and the peak is growing back.

9

Why do volcanoes erupt?

The inside of the Earth is being heated up all the time. Volcanoes are nature's way of letting heat escape and cooling down the Earth.

Hot rocks

The Earth is not a solid, unbroken mass. Instead, it is made up of several layers. We live on the thin outer layer of solid rock called the **crust**. This is about 30 kilometres thick on land, but only about 6–10 kilometres thick under the oceans. Underneath the crust is a thick layer of hot rocks called the **mantle**. In places, the mantle has melted to form **magma**, which flows like sticky tar.

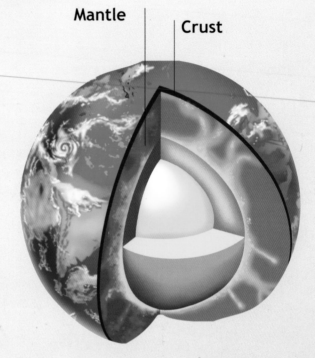

Mantle   Crust

● The layers of the Earth.

● Red-hot magma erupts through the Earth's crust and flows downhill.

Volcano

Crust

Plates

Mantle

Escaping Magma

- Magma pushes against the Earth's crust until it finds a weak spot.

Moving plates

The crust is not a seamless layer around the Earth. Instead, it is made up of smaller sections called **plates**, which fit together like a jigsaw puzzle. The plates float on liquid magma that is constantly pushing up against the plates. Wherever there is a weak spot, the magma rises towards the surface, creating a volcano. Usually, this is a place close to where two plates meet.

DATA FILE

- There are seven major plates and many minor plates.

- Plates move from a few mm to about 13 cm a year.

- A plate moving at 5 cm a year will travel about 50 km in a million years.

- Plates are about 100 km thick.

- Plates can push into each other, pull away from each other, slide by each other or one plate can slide over the top of another.

- Most volcanoes and earthquakes occur where plates meet.

Mauna Loa

Some of the world's most beautiful islands were made by volcanoes, and this is true of the Hawaiian Islands in the Pacific Ocean. These islands are actually the tips of undersea mountains that were formed by volcanoes.

Mauna Loa erupting in 1984.

Name: Mauna Loa
Location: Hawaii
Height: 4,170 metres
Type: Shield cone
Eruption: 1984
Fatalities: None

● By sampling Mauna Loa's lava, scientists study changes in its behaviour.

Largest volcano

There are several volcanoes on the island of Hawaii. One of them, Mauna Loa, is the world's largest active volcano. It last erupted in 1984. When Mauna Loa erupts, it produces hot, runny lava that flows long distances before it cools and hardens. This is the reason that this volcano has gently sloping sides and, at 100 kilometres across, is extremely wide. At its top, or summit, Mauna Loa has a huge oval crater, the world's second largest crater. Mauna Loa, and its neighbouring Kilauea volcano, are visited by many tourists each year. Visitors can approach the rim of the volcanoes and look directly down into their craters.

Time to escape

Mauna Loa is a fairly quiet volcano. Although the lava it produces is destructive and can do immense damage to crops and livestock, it is slow-moving. The number of human lives this volcano has claimed is low, as people usually have time to pack their possessions and leave the area.

Inside a volcano

Most volcanoes occur where the Earth's plates crash together or break apart. Two-thirds of the world's active volcanoes are found around the edge of the Pacific Ocean, where several plates meet.

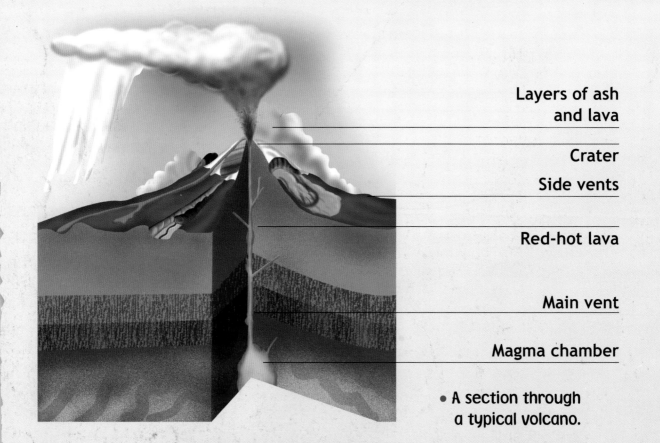

Layers of ash and lava

Crater

Side vents

Red-hot lava

Main vent

Magma chamber

• A section through a typical volcano.

Magma and lava

Where the Earth's crust is thin, magma rises and forms large underground pools, called **magma reservoirs**.

As the magma collects, it presses against the surrounding rock. When it finds a weak spot, the magma forces its way up a **vent** and bursts to the surface to form a volcano.

Volcanic bombs

Although magma reaches the surface through a volcano's main crater, other openings can appear in the sides of a volcano. When blasted high into the air, lava may harden into huge lumps of rock called volcanic bombs.

Hot-spot volcanoes

Not all volcanoes are found near the edges of the Earth's plates. The Hawaiian Islands, for example, which were made by volcanoes, are 3,200 kilometres from the nearest plate edges. Scientists believe that rising magma can push a hole in a weak part of the Earth's crust, known as a hot spot, to form a volcano.

- Tanzania's Mount Kilimanjaro is one of the world's largest inactive volcanoes.

DATA FILE

- Stromboli, a volcano off the coast of Italy, has been active since records began more than 2,500 years ago. It erupts about once every 20 minutes.

- More than 80 per cent of the Earth's surface was produced by volcanoes. Gases from volcanoes formed the Earth's atmosphere.

- Huge lightning flashes are sometimes seen during volcanic eruptions. It is believed that the millions of hot particles rubbing together produce giant sparks.

- In 1963, fishermen off the coast of Iceland watched a mound of black, steaming rock slowly rise up from the sea. Over the years, a new volcanic island, now called Surtsey, formed at this spot.

Paricutin

Paricutin is famous for giving scientists an incredible opportunity. For the first time, it was possible to study a volcano from when it was formed until the time it died.

Name: Paricutin
Location: South-western Mexico
Height: 2,809 metres
Type: Cinder cone
Eruption: 1943–1952
Fatalities: 3

New volcano

In February 1943, a 50 centimetre-deep crack opened in a cornfield near the Mexican village of Paricutin. The ground rose by two metres and a thick cloud of smoke and ashes shot upwards. A few hours later, red-hot rocks were being hurled high into the air. A new volcano was forming. By the same time the following day, the cornfield was covered by a cone of ashes 50 metres high. Seven days later, it was 150 metres high.

• The eruption of Paricutin began in 1943 and ended in 1952.

● Church towers are all that is visible above the lava that buried Paricutin.

Crater rim

After a year, the cone was 336 metres high. The new **cinder cone** volcano erupted for another eight years, throwing out about a billion tonnes of lava. In February 1952, it stopped as suddenly as it had begun. By then, the crater rim stood 410 metres above the remains of the cornfield.

DATA FILE

- Paricutin is considered by some to be one of the Seven Natural Wonders of the World.

- Paricutin is one of a chain of volcanoes that stretch more than 1,100 km across the breadth of southern Mexico.

- Paricutin is one of several hundred volcanoes in the area that have erupted in recent times.

- Unlike many other volcanoes, Paricutin erupted from just a single vent.

- The hardened lava from Paricutin now covers about 26 sq. km, while the dust and ash from it is spread over 52 sq. km.

● Scientists collecting samples from Paricutin's cinder cone.

Nevado del Ruiz

It is a fact that mud, as well as hot volcanic ash and lava, can be fatal. Many people died from the deadly mudflows that resulted when Colombia's snow-capped volcano, Nevado del Ruiz, erupted.

Name: Nevado del Ruiz
Location: Central Colombia
Height: 5,321 metres
Type: Composite cone
Eruption: 1985
Fatalities: 23,000

Warning ignored

Local people called Nevado del Ruiz the Sleeping Lion because it had been **dormant**, or sleeping, for nearly 150 years. In November 1984, however, the volcano began puffing steam and ash. Scientists were worried and warned that a disaster was possible. They recommended that evacuation plans be prepared. The Government took little notice of the warning as the volcano was a long way from any towns or villages.

● The main active crater of Nevado del Ruiz volcano.

• Although Nevado del Ruiz is near the Equator, its summit is extremely high and permanently covered in snow.

Black mud

In the afternoon of 13 November 1985, there was a small eruption and Nevado del Ruiz began to throw out fountains of ash. The main eruption began in the evening. Over a period of about three hours, 20 million cubic metres of hot ashes and rocks poured out of the vent.

This covered the volcano's snow cap as well as the small glacier that ran down one side. Beneath the blanket of hot ashes and rocks, the snow and ice around the summit of Nevado del Ruiz quickly melted. This caused a torrent of slimy, black mud to pour down a river valley on the northern slopes of the volcano.

Lethal lahars

Wave after wave of the mudflows, some of which were 40 metres thick, raced down the sides of the volcano at speeds of 50 km/h or more. Boulders, trees, bridges and people in the path of the mudflows were swept away or buried. The mudflows, called **lahars**, headed towards the small town of Armero, some 74 kilometres away. Picking up water and mud from the river valleys, the deadly lahars grew in size as they moved away from the volcano.

• The town of Armero was buried in mud, produced when hot ash mixed with water from melting ice and snow.

Armero destroyed

It took only two and a half hours for the mudflows to reach Armero. A warning had been sent out, but it did not reach the people in time and Armero was destroyed. Only 100 of its 5,000 houses remained intact. Amazingly, the cemetery survived unscathed. Altogether, the lahars killed 23,000 people, which included 90 per cent of the population of Armero. There were thousands of deaths in surrounding villages, and many pets and farm animals died.

A survivor is rescued by helicopter from dangerous mud.

Avoiding disasters

Some good came from the disaster. The United States Geological Survey organised a team of scientists and provided them with a portable volcano observatory, which can be sent anywhere in the world where a volcano shows signs of awakening. A warning could then be given so that disasters such as that at Nevado del Ruiz would not happen again. On Nevado del Ruiz itself, detectors have been put in place. These devices can warn of any movement that may result in a lahar.

DATA FILE

- The Nevado del Ruiz tragedy marked the second worst volcanic disaster of the 20th century.

- As well as the 23,000 human deaths, about 15,000 animals died.

- Armero had been built on the top of old mudflows from the volcano.

- In Armero, the mud destroyed two hospitals, 50 schools, 58 factories and 343 shops and offices.

- About 60 per cent of the area's farm animals and 30 per cent of the rice crop were destroyed.

- Many people who only had minor cuts died when their wounds became infected by the dirty mud.

Volcano shapes

The hill, or mountain, around the vent of a volcano is called a cone. The three main types of cone are the cinder cone, **shield cone** and composite cone.

Cinder cone

When volcanoes erupt with great violence, burning gases, hot ash and **cinders** are forced high into the sky. The eruption builds up a steep cone of ashes and cinders around the volcano's vent. This results in a cinder cone volcano, such as Paricutin in Mexico.

Shield cone

When lava is runny, it spreads out around the crater before hardening. The lava forms a gently sloping volcano, like a shield lying on the ground. This is why a volcano such as Mauna Loa is called a shield cone.

Composite cone

If a volcano erupts quietly and then violently, a tall, composite cone is produced. This is made up of layers of different materials. Mount St Helens in the United States is a composite cone.

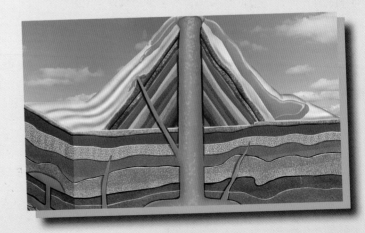

- Mount Pinatubo in the Philippines, a composite cone volcano, erupted in 1991 with tremendous force. Thousands of buildings were destroyed.

Active, extinct and dormant volcanoes

Although a few volcanoes erupt all the time, most only erupt now and then. A volcano that erupts is called active. Some volcanoes, such as Mount Kilimanjaro in Tanzania and Mount Shasta in the United States, have not erupted for thousands of years and are said to be **extinct**. Other volcanoes are dormant, or sleeping. It is not always easy to tell whether a volcano is dormant or extinct. Scientists thought that Eldfell volcano on the island of Heimaey, near Iceland, was extinct. In 1973, however, it erupted violently and destroyed 300 buildings.

DATA FILE

- Argentina's Aconcagua is the highest **extinct volcano** in the world. It is 6,960 m high.

- Ecuador's Cotopaxi is one of the tallest active volcanoes on Earth. This composite cone is 5,911 m high.

- The world's largest **dormant volcano** is Haleakala on Maui, one of the Hawaiian Islands. It is 3,048 m high.

- At 5,895 m, Tanzania's extinct volcano Mount Kilimanjaro is the highest free-standing mountain in the world.

- About 60 per cent of the world's volcanoes have composite cones.

Lake Nyos

Lake Nyos is perched high on a mountain in Cameroon, West Africa. Unlike most other lakes, Lake Nyos fills the crater of a volcano that last erupted several centuries ago.

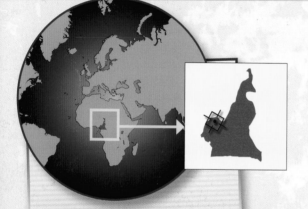

Name: Lake Nyos
Location: North-western Cameroon, West Africa
Height: 3,011 metres
Type: Crater lake
Eruption: 1986
Fatalities: 1,700

Danger in the depths

The waters of Lake Nyos hide a deadly secret. Deep below, carbon dioxide slowly bubbles out from tiny holes in blocked volcanic vents at the bottom of the lake. The surface of the lake is warmed by the hot sun, but 200 metres down the water is cold and thick with the gas.

- About 200m under the surface of Lake Nyos, carbon dioxide seeps into its cold waters.

Deadly cloud

On the evening of 21 August 1986, carbon dioxide gas at the bottom of Lake Nyos suddenly gushed upwards and formed a huge cloud above the surface of the lake. As carbon dioxide is heavier than other gases in the air, the cloud hugged the ground and rushed down to the villages below, reaching speeds of 50 km/h. In the villages, cooking fires were put out and people suffocated in their beds. In the village of Subum, 10 kilometres from the lake, patients on the first floor of the hospital were unharmed, while those downstairs were suffocated. Altogether, the gas cloud killed 1,700 people, 6,000 cattle and countless birds and mammals.

• These cows were just of a few of the thousands of domestic animals killed by the deadly clouds of gas from Lake Nyos.

Safety pipes

Scientists have now placed plastic pipes in Lake Nyos to circulate its water. This allows small amounts of carbon dioxide gas to bubble out and escape safely into the air.

Yellowstone Park

Situated in the border areas of the American states of Wyoming, Montana and Idaho, Yellowstone National Park is famous for the hundreds of **geysers**, **hot springs** and bubbling **mudpots** found within its boundaries.

Name: Old Faithful
Location: Yellowstone National Park, Wyoming, USA
Height: Column of water 30–55 metres high
Type: Geysers
Eruption: About every 66 to 80 minutes

Giant caldera

Almost the whole of Yellowstone National Park lies in a huge basin called a **caldera**. This was formed about 600,000 years ago when a gigantic ancient volcano erupted and then collapsed. The magma chamber that formed the original volcano is still present, about 6 kilometres below the surface. Underneath Yellowstone's caldera is a hot spot that is slowly moving up and down at the rate of about 3.5 centimetres per year.

● Terraces at Mammoth Hot Springs, in Yellowstone Park. These form when hot water streams down a slope, evaporates and leaves behind dissolved chemicals, which then harden.

Steaming fumaroles

Above the Yellowstone magma chamber there are over 300 geysers. This is more than anywhere else in the world. The most famous geyser is Old Faithful. There are also about 10,000 hot springs, mudpots and steaming **fumaroles**. Like Old Faithful, they are heated by the magma chamber below.

Old Faithful

On average, Old Faithful erupts every 66 to 80 minutes. For ten minutes before it erupts, this predictable geyser bubbles and splutters. It then shoots up a column of steam and boiling water between 30 and 55 metres into the air.

- Old Faithful Geyser in Wyoming, United States, has been erupting almost every hour for many hundreds of years.

DATA FILE

- When Old Faithful erupts, 45,000 lt of hot water are discharged along with billowing steam.

- The average height of one of Old Faithful's eruptions is 44 m.

- Each eruption of Old Faithful lasts between 1.5 and 5 minutes.

- In Yellowstone National Park, the water temperature at 200 m below the surface is 200 °C.

- There is another geyser in Yellowstone Park, called Steamboat, which produces the world's highest spurt of water and steam. This sometimes reaches 122 m.

Lakes, geysers and hot springs

Lakes, known as crater lakes, can form in volcanic craters. In some areas, such as Yellowstone National Park, geysers, hot springs, mudpots and fumaroles heated by hot rocks underground are also found.

Crater lakes

We have already seen that Lake Nyos was formed in the crater of a volcano. High in the mountains of Oregon, in the United States, is another circular lake nearly 600 metres deep. This lake is known as Crater Lake. The lake was formed when the sides of the volcano collapsed inwards after a series of eruptions. Rainwater then filled the large cavity, or caldera.

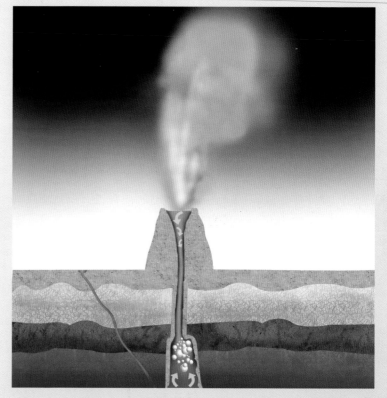

• How a geyser is formed.

Bubbling mudpots

Geysers are formed when water from the surface seeps down, collects underground and is heated by the hot rocks. A jet of steam and boiling water then shoots high into the air with great force. When enough water has seeped back down through the ground, the process is repeated. In some places, sulphuric acid, sometimes found near a geyser, dissolves the surrounding rock and produces a slimy, bubbling mudpot.

Converting steam

As well as being popular tourist attractions, geysers and hot springs have other uses. In Iceland, for example, water from hot springs is used to heat homes, swimming pools and greenhouses. In other countries, such as Italy, Mexico and New Zealand, water from hot springs is piped to power stations to be turned into steam. The steam turns the turbines that generate electricity.

- At 589 m, Crater Lake is the second deepest lake in the USA. It occupies a crater 14 km wide, which was formed by a series of overlapping volcanoes.

DATA FILE

- The 22 km wide Ngorongo Crater, in Tanzania, is covered with dry, grassy plains that are home to more than 30,000 wild animals.

- In 1864, a hotel in Oregon, in the United States, began to heat rooms using energy from underground hot springs.

- In Iceland, tropical fruits such as bananas and pineapples are grown in greenhouses heated by hot water from geysers.

- The first **geothermal power** station opened in Italy in 1911.

- Geothermal power is now used in more than 20 countries.

Glossary

active volcano a volcano that erupts from time to time

caldera a huge, bowl-shaped cavity formed when a volcano collapses into its empty magma chamber after it has erupted

cinder a small piece of partly burned material

cinder cone a volcano with a steep cone of ashes and cinders. Cinder cone volcanoes usually erupt with great violence

composite cone a tall, cone-shaped volcano built up by many eruptions. It is made of layers of lava and layers of ashes and cinders

cone the hill or mountain formed by a volcano

crater the funnel-shaped hole at the top of a volcano

crust the Earth's outer layer of rock, on which we live

dormant volcano a volcano that is resting or inactive, not erupting

erupt when magma is forced out of a weak spot in the Earth's crust, forming a volcano

extinct volcano a volcano that is no longer active

fumarole a small opening in the ground through which hot gases can escape from deep inside the Earth

geothermal power the energy produced using the steam from water that is heated by the red-hot rocks beneath the surface of the Earth

geyser a hot spring that throws a jet of hot water and steam into the air from time to time

hot spring a stream of hot water coming from the ground

lahar a muddy flow of water mixed with ash and other material from an erupting volcano. A lahar is often called a mudflow

lava the molten rock that comes out of a volcano

magma the hot molten, or liquid, rock formed in the Earth's mantle, just below the crust

magma reservoir a large pool of magma beneath the surface of the Earth

mantle the layer of rock below the Earth's crust and above the core. The mantle is thought to be so hot that some of the rocks have melted and are a sticky liquid

mudpot a pool of hot, bubbling mud, which is usually white or grey in colour

plates the sections of the Earth's crust. The slow, steady movements of the plates cause changes in the Earth's surface

shield cone a gently sloping volcano, formed by liquid lava that has spread out around the crater of the volcano

tsunami a large sea wave, usually caused by an earthquake on the sea bed

vent the opening in a volcano from which lava, gases, ashes and cinders erupt

Index

Webfinder

www.fema.gov/kids/volcano.htm
A simple and friendly site with basic information about volcanoes

http://volcano.und.nodak.edu/
An up-to-date site for children, which includes volcano myths and legends from around the world as well as games and puzzles

www.learner.org/interactives/volcanoes/entry.html
This site provides information on how we can predict volcanic eruptions and how best to deal with them

http://education.usgs.gov/common/primary.htm#volcanoes
A site containing educational resources for teachers of young children. The site includes live views of volcanoes around the world